Love Letters

Love Letters

PSALMS FOR ALL HUMANS

John T. Bainbridge

RESOURCE *Publications* · Eugene, Oregon

LOVE LETTERS
Psalms for All Humans

Copyright © 2022 John T. Bainbridge. All rights reserved. Except for brief quotations in critical publications or reviews, no part of this book may be reproduced in any manner without prior written permission from the publisher. Write: Permissions, Wipf and Stock Publishers, 199 W. 8th Ave., Suite 3, Eugene, OR 97401.

Resource Publications
An Imprint of Wipf and Stock Publishers
199 W. 8th Ave., Suite 3
Eugene, OR 97401

www.wipfandstock.com

PAPERBACK ISBN: 978-1-6667-3850-6
HARDCOVER ISBN: 978-1-6667-9928-6
EBOOK ISBN: 978-1-6667-9929-3

APRIL 14, 2022 8:14 AM

Scriptures taken from the Holy Bible, New International Version®, NIV®. Copyright © 1973, 1978, 1984, 2011 by Biblica, Inc.™ Used by permission of Zondervan. All rights reserved worldwide. www.zondervan.com The "NIV" and "New International Version" are trademarks registered in the United States Patent and Trademark Office by Biblica, Inc.™

Dedicated to my two pearls of great price, Jeremy and Fiona

Contents

Introduction | ix

Psalm 1. "Blessed." | 1
Psalm 2. Love as the legacy of nations. | 2
Psalm 3. Love is safe. | 3
Psalm 4. Love in our DNA. | 4
Psalm 5. What Love is not. | 5
Psalm 6. Love through pain. | 7
Psalm 7. The Love judge. | 8
Psalm 8. The Love ambassadors. | 10
Psalm 9. Love, my superpower. | 11
Psalm 10. Love not indifferent to manipulation! | 13
Psalm 11. Stay and look Love in the eye. | 15
Psalm 12. Love! Enough is enough! | 16
Psalm 13. Discovering Love in the mirror. | 17
Psalm 14. Party invitation for the exploited. | 18
Psalm 15. The guest list. | 19
Psalm 16. Journeying with Love along the path. | 20
Psalm 17. Love, saving the real me. | 21
Psalm 18. We got this! | 23
Psalm 19. Love's loveliness infiltrating me. | 28
Psalm 20. May things go well for us. | 30

Psalm 21. Smiling champions. | 31

Psalm 22. Public humiliation and the draft public announcement. | 33

Psalm 23. Love, my guide, my host. | 37

Psalm 24. Letting go. | 38

Psalm 25. My Love GPS, navigating me out of trouble. | 40

Psalm 26. Integrity Trail Path. | 43

Psalm 27. Strong hearts. | 44

Psalm 28. Energy resource. | 46

Psalm 29. Love's voice, volume turned up to 10. | 48

Psalm 30. Dawn never fails. | 49

Psalm 31. Empowerment for the glass hammer. | 51

Psalm 32. Fessing up, unlocking responsibility. | 54

Psalm 33. From Love tunes to worldwide advance. | 56

Psalm 34. Serious long-term joint rescuing. | 58

Psalm 35. Love's on their case. | 61

Psalm 36. Keep shining, keep resisting. | 64

Psalm 37. Good versus evil. | 66

Psalm 38. Finding harmony in the dissonance. | 70

Psalm 39. Vanishing vapor. | 72

Psalm 40. Love's rescue made available in its own time. | 74

Psalm 41. When body, mind, and reputation are under attack. | 77

Appendix: "Accurate" Bible Translations | 79

Introduction

CHURCH BIBLE STUDY NIGHT (*groan*). "Let us try to express the passage in our own words," suggests the meeting leader. But what are we supposed to do with "iniquities," "apostles," "gentiles," "rebuke" or even "Lord" Christian attendees might secretly be wondering?! If even they need the religious language decoding, might it be time to ask who the Bible is even for and why even bother with it? If we are honest, even though many may find parts of "God's Word" provide spiritual insight, the Bible itself seems to need constant repackaging and reformulation to make sense even to the faithful.

Bible translation is on the verge of waking up to a huge challenge: with declining interest in the Christian spiritual message across the Western world, many would not even consider it as a primary source of spiritual insight and guidance. So, how might the Bible be rebranded? Not as yet another attempt to be more "modern," but as a collection of potentially life-changing texts available to all humans, wherever they are, whatever language they speak and *whatever their religious or spiritual outlook*? Somehow, perhaps this "religious book" might need to dispense with its black, leather-bound image in order to keep sharing its sacred, earthy, and universal message with everyone seeking a deeper understanding about life.

In many ways, it is in the Hebrew wisdom texts like the Psalms where this question climaxes, where arguably we have the fullest biblical engagement of the whole question of what it means to be human, regardless of our background and affiliations. Join us and share with us an extraordinary paradigm shift as we imagine Love truly personified,[1] connecting readers who are looking for a deeper and more solid direction

---

1. "For who or what could we call 'God' or 'higher power', except LOVE itself? Could we ground our lives in anything else, anything even half as solid?" (18:31)

Introduction

in their lives by building on ancient wisdom, minus the entanglement of religious Christian language.

Have *you* ever found biblical language bothersome, irrelevant, or even repulsive? A variety of reactions exist and are completely normal. We are in urgent need of translations and paraphrases of ancient wisdom texts that help reconnect, expand, and enrich our lives in fresh ways, transcending barbed religious dividing lines and painful memories where necessary. It is our strong hope that this non-religious offering of the Psalms might have a place in that larger project and be of direct benefit to you. *Love Letters* is carefully designed as a thematic translation with a focus on humanity as healthy carriers of a transformative power we simply call "Love." Is this just cheap cultural interpolation? Or does it build on a foundation of Judeo-Christian tradition spanning millennia?

These traditions indeed go right back to the earliest texts themselves and legitimize two key steps in our efforts to lift the message free of religious obstacles. Here you will not find any assumptions requiring belief in a being called "God." If that's a dealbreaker for you, you might ask yourself the question, "what do I understand by that word anyway?" The Bible itself provides another way of understanding God, our first key step:

> Dear friends, let us love one another, for love comes from God. Everyone who loves has been born of God and knows God. Whoever does not love does not know God, because *God is love.*[2]

The New Testament writer John was convinced: "God" is Love in its very essence. If for you like many others, "God" is or could be also your higher power, both intimate and transcendent, maybe Love personified, then maybe we humans share more ground with each other than we realize! Atheists, secularists, humanists, Christians, Muslims, Jews, Buddhists, Hindus, animists . . . we may *all* find more compelling spiritual truth and insight here than we ever dreamed possible. Maybe as the conversation continues, we could agree that anchoring Love at the center is what gives relief, salvation, and meaning to all our short human lives.

Here is the second key step:

> No one has ever seen God; but if we love one another, *God (Love) lives in us*[3]

---

2. 1 John 4:7–8, italics added
3. 1 John 4:12, italics and parentheses added

Introduction

This means the Psalms can also be rendered with the conviction that God (Love) is powerfully resident *within* human beings, rather than summoned into situations from some outer stratosphere. The ultimate and perfect example of that for the early Christian communities was their unlikely hero, Jesus Christ, "God-made-flesh." Jesus tells one of his followers, Philip, that anyone who has seen him has also seen "the Father" and that he and "the Father" are "in" one another.[4] However, way before Jesus and the early Christian-era thinkers reinforced the idea of God's indwelling, writers from within the Judeo-Christian tradition had always attempted to understand God in very human ways, contributing perhaps to why we see so much anthropomorphism even in older Jewish texts like the Psalms (written originally in Hebrew). So in short, when the Hebrew God acts or is called to act, *Love Letters* will generally describe that action as a sort of partnership between the person themselves and Love at work within them, a gracious empowerment of a person whose life flows with love.

This extraordinary revelation of an indwelling divine presence is not an isolated Christian notion; it has been picked up throughout history ever since too. In the thirteenth century, for instance, St. Clare of Assissi encouraged her sisters to "place yourself before the mirror," "let the Light mirror you," and "Look upon the mirror [of perfect love] each day." Her Sufi Muslim contemporary, Jalal Rumi, said, "Your task is not to seek for love, but merely to seek and find all the barriers within yourself that you have built against it."

So we see it as very appropriate, thrilling even, to reinforce the idea of divine Love showing itself through the Psalmist's own humanity. As a human being reading this, maybe you too might glimpse Love in you, able to extend through you to impact your mind, your body, your facial expressions, your home, your relationships, your work, and your world—if you are willing.

In addition to these two broad steps (that "God" can be Love personified and that this is also a power residing in and released through human beings), a range of other cultural equivalences have been adopted. This is so we can hold firmly to the goal of communicating the ideas and themes into a non-religious reader's world. We will let you discover these choices as you read on, but please note that traditional Psalm verse numbering has been largely maintained for ease of reference to mainstream translations, albeit with some portions grouped.

4. John 4:9–10.

Introduction

This grouping is worth briefly explaining. Ancient Hebrew poetry can be a little confusing with themes sometimes rushing to and fro between the past, present, and future. Not only that, but the Psalmists' addressees also often switch rapidly, between God, their own soul, the faithful believers, "the nations", and so on. This was unlikely, however, to have been confusing in their time and context—they were building up a multifaceted and seamless picture best communicated through this kind of strong, sacred, and poetic imagery and movement. The necessary reorganization of the material in the mind of the ancient reader and listener was part of their interaction with and appropriation of the community's great divine story and hope. However, for communicating in modern more linear western cultures, we have on occasion elected to reorder the material slightly to allow for a greater sense of flow, while also flagging changes of addressee where it may enhance clarity for the reader.

Regardless of your background and culture, we cannot wait to hear how the Psalms have impacted you, maybe even as Love emerges as a cornerstone of your own journey. We hope you will agree with our early readers (some of whom have no particular love for the Bible) that they can be highly accessible. One reader commented that "the recontextualization is absolutely amazing."

But credit is not to this author or even his wonderful consultancy team—it is to the Psalmists themselves (there were several). If these texts work, then we can put it down to the fact that they are about us humans continuously endeavoring to transcend deep suffering and to journey more freely via a deep sense of abandonment to Love's authorizing authority. On that journey our hosts will have us visit a swathe of experiences, speaking to much of the pain, frustration, hope, happiness, gratitude, disappointment, passion, fantasy, and reality we experience in this short life. It is through the honest expression of human experience in relation to humanity's great wrestling with and search for Love, that transformation became possible for the Psalmists, and for many, many centuries of readers ever since. I gratefully add my own name to that long list of people being changed by the Psalms and dearly hope you can do the same.

A debt of gratitude for this work is also owed especially to Kirk Woodyard whose reflective input, enthusiasm and encouragement for this project have been priceless and tireless. His own work on Psalm 40 also so impacted my draft that I would consider this dear friend cowriter of that

Introduction

chapter. Furthermore, my father Ian Bainbridge provided some excellent editorial input and encouragement. The overall list of encouragers is quite long, however, and without the winds of encouragement in our sails we can end up woefully adrift—that has been my experience anyway! My sincere thanks then extends to everyone who has accompanied me on this journey.

John T. Bainbridge

loveletters2022@outlook.com

Psalm 1. "Blessed."

¹⁻³ Some humans are passionate about life,
      Lives framed by Love itself.
  They meditate on Love's way
      During the day, during the night.
  Free from the influence of doing harm,
      Stepping outside that mentality completely,
  They would not even consider
      Stooping to ridicule.

These kinds of human are like healthy trees planted by streams of water.
      Just as every season they give up their fruit,
    Life coursing through the veins of their radiantly green leaves,
      So too these people experience life and growth from their roots.

Some call this sort of life "blessed."

⁴ That is not, however, how life pans out
      For those profiting at others' expense.
  They are like sandcastles at the water's edge
      That the tide will soon erase.

⁵ These folk will not hold up to public scrutiny
      Or attend community development meetings.

⁶ So, while Love is intimately at work shaping lives for the good,
  Profiteering gain games will one day be game over, period.

Psalm 2. LOVE as the legacy of nations.

Why would nations and states waste their time,
>Competing and planning separatist breakaways?
² Governments vote and heads of state gather,
>Yet it's all LOVE-less, they're undermining humanity's cause.
Since LOVE is our cause—it chose us!—
>They undermine us directly.
³ You can sense their scheming:
>"Let's break free, do our own thing,
For too long now we have paid—
>Suffered—the price of the 'LOVE' agenda."

⁴ I sense a divine hilarity stirring in response,
>As if anything else could define and direct our nations' paths!
⁵ One day the joke'll be over, LOVE'll stop them in their tracks,
>They'll cower before its greatness. They'll get it.
⁶ They'll get we are still empowered. By what authority?
>By LOVE itself,
Helping us lead the great program,
>Increasing LOVE's territory and influence.

⁷ So, let me share what LOVE has taught me:
>"You are my children,
>>Today I have become your parent.
⁸ Keep me as your purpose and your inheritance is assured,
>>This is your world.
⁹ You will exercise your power with authority,
>>Smashing to smithereens any resistance to LOVE's great cause!"

¹⁰ Therefore, heads of state, wise up.
>Governments globally, watch out.
¹¹ LOVE needs respect, awe,
>But releases huge joy.
¹² So embracing our passion,
>Don't suddenly frustrate LOVE's advance, losing your way.

All of us—everyone trusting LOVE's way is the safe way—
>We will count ourselves "blessed."

Psalm 3. LOVE is safe.

A poem ascribed to a dad forced to flee his own son

Good God! There are so many people who have it in for me!
>How many of them are there?
>>² I could easily overhear them talking about me:
>>>"What good are his LOVE values to him now?"

Pause

³ But you, LOVE, are literally a shield around me,
>You make me shine, pick me up.
>>⁴ I urgently dial in to you and we connect
>>>At that precious sacred space within.

Pause

To Diary:

⁵ I lie down.
>I sleep well.
>LOVE has recharged me during my time of rest
>>To keep me going in the day.
>>⁶ I realize I can be confident facing these overwhelming pressures,
>>>Attacks raining in from all sides, outside and in.

To LOVE, back in the fray:

⁷ I'm yelling:
>"You're my higher power, get me through this!
>Crush every single horrid word and thought about me,
>>Put this bad mouthing shop out of business permanently."

⁸ Yes. Security is gained through LOVE;
>May we as LOVE's people count ourselves "blessed."

Pause

Psalm 4. LOVE in our DNA.

Dear LOVE, connect with me again as I reach into you,
    My perfectly good higher power.
    You've relieved me from my anxiety before,
        So please help us reconnect.

To my fellow humans:

[2] How long, folks, will you reduce my pride and joy
    To an embarrassment, an optional human value?
    How much longer will you be talking up your pipe dreams,
        Endlessly chasing rainbows?

Pause

[3] We must understand LOVE's chosen *us*,
    Embedding itself even deep within our DNA.
    Getting this, when I go "Answer me when I call,"
        LOVE is there, LOVE connects.

[4] Living for LOVE does not mean anger is banned,
    Just that it's channeled for good, not harm.
    Things are cooling down now,
        Finding time to pause,
    Checking where our hearts are at,
        Being still.

[5] It is also good being ready to make sacrifices,
    Trusting in LOVE in us to make the stretch.

To LOVE:

[6] So, LOVE, if people start questioning,
    Can anything truly be *good*?
    Let your light in me
        Shine goodness through my face!

[7] At times like this I sense you fill my heart so full of happiness,
    Fuller than a child's joy on Christmas morning.
    [8] Now it's time for me to go to bed relaxed, ready for sleep,
        Knowing only you make me feel safe.

Psalm 5. What Love is not.

Dear Love, hear my words, these words,
      And the struggle exhaled in my sigh.
   [2-3] Listen to my yelp for help this morning:
      You're my higher power,
I defer to you entirely.
      I reach in, Love,
We connect,
      I pause,
The day yet to start,
      I just wait, expectantly.

[4-5] Neither darkness nor harm
      Float my higher power's boat,
All human harm unwelcome,
      We can't stand damaging behavior.
          Arrogance: blast it away.
          [6] Lying,
          Bloodletting,
          Shady dealing:
                All on the shoot-to-kill list!

[7] So, thank you so much because it's out of your vast kindness
      I get to access your presence,
I let this awe take over my core
      In this sacred space where we embrace.
[8] Lead me in your good way,
      Make it clear what I need to do,
Iron out my creases,
      My undermining distractions.

[9] Ok, so about those.
      We cannot trust a single word those voices say
Because all they are about is damaging us.
      Somehow, they still flatter people, kidding them,
          Even though their words lack true vitality.
   [10] Love, call them out! You have the power.
      Let their plans blow up in their faces.

>   Have those rebel voices leave office,
>> Leave *town* for good.
>
> [11] As for those protected folk,
>> Protected by you,
>> Let them just be so happy, year in year out,
>>> Expressing their joy.
>> They love LOVE's name,
>>> So reward their trust with such a sweet happiness.
>
> [12] Without any doubt whatsoever, you, LOVE,
>> You do bring good to those who are good,
>> You do work things out for them,
>>> Protecting them from entering pain.

Psalm 6. Love through pain.

Dear Love, please let me off the hook,
    I have not been true to you and my true self.
  I do not deserve you,
    I imagine you almost angry with me.
  [2] Give me another chance,
    I am not strong right now.
  Love—restore my body,
    Each and every aching bone,
  [3] Love—touch my mind,
    Wound up in so much tension . . .
        But when will I be fixed?!
  [4] Please return and fix me up,
    Let undying Love get me through this.

[5] Maybe there is something in it for you too!
        No-one is cheering you on from the morgue, are they?!

[6] Gosh, I am so tired out by my own self-pity,
    I have cried so much in bed my pillow is soaked through.
  [7] My face looks drained and my eyes stare out blankly,
    My brain just too fried by my mental struggles.

[8] Hey, you, engineers of human harm—
    Keep your distance.
  My SOS bottle sailed my tears,
    Washed up on Love's shores,
  [9] And it was read.
    Loud and clear.
  I do not deserve rescuing,
    But Love has reached into my world.
  [10] So, all my negative forces,
    In a world of trouble,
  Ashamed and exposed,
    They turn and scarper.

Psalm 7. The LOVE judge.

¹⁻² Dear LOVE, you are my higher power,
    I am safest under your protection.
There's a target on my head.
    Empower me.
Without your partnership,
    I'm beaten to a pulp, helplessly alone.

³ LOVE, you are my higher power,
    If I've messed up, not yet owned up,
⁴ Perhaps harming the harmless,
    Maybe taking something I'd no right to,
⁵ Then I'm ready to face the consequences:

    → My personal life exposed,
    → Publicly humiliated,
    → Utterly crushed.

Pause

⁶ As for my enemies,
    I feel LOVE in me frustrated by their rage,
Wake up then, LOVE, rise up within me!
    Help us deal with them rightly.

⁷ As you mingle, LOVE,
    Providing the atmosphere in the courts,
As judgements are formed,
    Reinstill that sense of serving LOVE's higher cause.
⁸ Ultimately you, LOVE itself, are the judge of all humans,
    Justice LOVE, Chief Judge,
Have me judged according to my integrity,
    The good alive within me.
⁹ Power of pure goodness,
    Infiltrating our minds and emotions,
Bring the root causes of violence to an end,
    Reaffirm all that is good in us.

To Diary:

¹⁰ My defense: my judge has full authority in my life—
    This is how healthy human hearts stay safe.
    ¹¹ Love is a good judge,
        Whose clear voice sternly opposes the chaos every time.
    ¹²⁻¹³ If Justice Love's voice goes unheeded,
        Stronger measures may be needed—
The darts of public ridicule,
    The isolation of zero-trust,
The shame of disrespect:
    They all bite back real hard.

¹⁴ Some people's minds go for a dark magic,
    Conjuring up harm, problems and lies.
    ¹⁵ It's a very poor choice,
        Sawing off the very branch they stand on,
    ¹⁶ The damage intended for others coming boomeranging back,
        Violently striking them on their own cocky head.

¹⁷ As for me, I am just so thankful for Justice Love,
    So good, so true.
    I know I'll always be singing the praises
        Of my Chief Justice.

Psalm 8. The LOVE ambassadors.

Dear LOVE, you are simply divine,
    Your awesomeness reaches right across the planet!
Further still, your excellence stretches up,
    Right across the glorious night sky.
[2] Since even babies and young kids
    Gurgle and shout your amazingness,
LOVE's opposing forces are left speechless,
    Their babbling muted.

[3] As my eyes drink in this night sky—moon, stars, and galaxies—
    I see your staggering beauty,
Your power on full display
    (I know you are somehow behind it all).
[4] I stumble backwards in wonder:
    What is it about us humans that you bother with us?
        Even to hang out with us?
[5-6] You honor us too with delegated responsibility,
    Official recognition,
Literally signing over the natural world
    To us little LOVE ambassadors.
[7] So livestock, domestic pets,
    The countless wild species of this world,
[8] Birds, fish or land creatures,
    The world's entire ecosystem, in fact,
        All are entrusted into our quivering hands.

[9] LOVE, our authority,
    News of your awesomeness
        Is reaching right across the planet!

Psalm 9. LOVE, my superpower.

Dear LOVE, I'll always be so thankful to you,
> I'll always be speaking out on behalf of your staggering impact.
² I'll always be so grateful and content in my LOVE space,
> I'll always be celebrating LOVE, my superpower.

³ My destructive influences are losing their grip,
> Melting away before your advance,
⁴ You vouch for me and my purpose,
> LOVE, you are recognized as the perfect judge of character.
⁵ So where programs deviate from your program,
> You sentence them for permanent removal.

Whether wayward individuals or whole bent systems,
> All are all brought to a crumbling ruin.
⁶ And time will pass and people forget
> The remaining rubble was once my sentenced enemy's citadel.

To LOVE's people:

⁷ LOVE is in office!
> Constantly steering us toward a fairer world,
⁸ Rolling out human rights everywhere—
> Deploying justice, regardless of culture and context.
⁹⁻¹⁰ More than that, LOVE is:

> → A safe house for the abused,
> → A strong resource when times are tough,
> → A name we can trust, never letting us down
>   (us your LOVE-seeking humans).

¹¹ So LOVE resident in our sacred spaces should be celebrated.
> We must profile the great good LOVE does,
¹² Like when LOVE reaches out to the abused
> Or holds people accountable for the pain,
>> For the trauma.

To Love:

¹³ Love, see how my demons are pummeling me!
        Give me a second chance please,
            Lift me out of this dead-end life.
   ¹⁴ Do this and my words will celebrate you,
        Your victory ringing out from my sacred space.

To Love's people:

¹⁵ One day whole nations will fall
        For the same traps they're setting others,
   Their power games ensnaring
        Their very own social fabric.
   ¹⁶ With Manipulation's plans clearly backfiring,
        Love will be recognized for the justice it brings.

Pause

¹⁷ Local manipulators right up to corrupted social systems,
        Everything and everyone abandoning Love is doomed.
   ¹⁸ But the cause and hopes of the needy, the oppressed,
        Will not be ignored, will not be squashed!

To Love:

¹⁹ Rise up, Love, please don't permit Love-less humanity to win.
        Let our entire society feel you and be held accountable!
   ²⁰ Let all humans be gripped by a daunting realization:
        We only have so long in this life!

Pause

Psalm 10. LOVE not indifferent to manipulation!

Dear LOVE, this is when I need you most so where ~~the hell~~,
    Ahem, *on Earth* are you?!

²Let me update you—manipulators are preying on the underprivileged,
    Let them be caught instead of their targets!
  ³They've absolutely no shame of their twisted desires,
    Encouraging humans to give up on LOVE, to be greedy.
⁴Their ego-governed minds, you see,
    Will not be seeking LOVE;
Although their brains are abuzz with thoughts,
    LOVE is never their focus.
  ⁵Somehow, their twisted ways not only exclude LOVE's path,
    But they seem to work out well!
And there those people sit,
    Smugly looking down from their high horses at us muck.
  ⁶"I'm unshakeable" is their morning mantra,
    Their twisted brains convinced their methods are bulletproof!

⁷Manipulators are basically liars, exuding veiled threats as they go,
    Trouble and harm lurking behind their every word.
  ⁸⁻¹⁰You can't see them coming,
    But their eyes are glued on their next victim.
Think of a stealthy lioness completely still as she waits,
    Just biding her time before lunging forward for the kill.
The poor prey hasn't a hope in hell,
    Brought crashing and bleeding to the ground,
        Totally at the mercy of the beast's hideous strength.

¹¹That's exactly how it is with manipulators,
    "Where is LOVE, anyway?" they say.
  "Even if LOVE is real,
    It's so out of touch with the real world."

¹²⁻¹³Why do these dodgy people get to think
    They can go it alone?
  "I'm my own boss" —
    So goes their smug go-to philosophy.
So involve yourself, LOVE,

> Please get stuck in,
> Keeping that divine hope alive,
>> Keeping us struggling humans in mind.

¹⁴ Thankfully, Love, you are only too aware of our issues,
>> Our suffering mobilizes you.
> We let go and release it all to Love's help,
>> Even us emotional orphans get empowered this way.

¹⁵ As for those oppressors causing pain and suffering—
>> Stop them in their tracks, debilitate them entirely.
> May they take the full responsibility they dodge
>> For the damage they have done.

¹⁶ Love you're in full charge here,
>> Always will be.
> Opposing forces have no jurisdiction in this place,
>> Steadily downsized until nothing is left.
> ¹⁷⁻¹⁸ The abused and emotional orphans are safeguarded,
>> Under protection orders against all future human oppression.
> Love's in tune with their hopes and cries,
>> Giving them the strength they need,
>>> Encouraging them.

Psalm 11. Stay and look Love in the eye.

I'm supposed to be the guy who trusts Love for everything,
> So why do I still hear a whispering in my soul:

"RUN! Run for your life,
> Abandon your home!

² Look at the bad stuff happening to good people,
> Even in the dead of night.

³ If our very foundations are detonated,
> What else can we do except scramble for safety?"

⁴ Well, Love is still here,
> Still owns the place we call "our lives,"

Closely watching over us all,
> Checking out each human heart.

⁵ Everything good is tested,
> But everything rotten (violence being the worst)
>> Is *unbearable* to the Love-filled heart.

⁶ Love will ensure human evils are exposed to hardship,
> Cataclysms if need be, whatever is proportionate.

⁷ Why? Because Love is about making the world right,
> So passionate about justice.

With our hearts in line,
> We look Love unashamedly in the eye.

Psalm 12. LOVE! Enough is enough!

Dear LOVE, intervene! No-one seems true to the good cause anymore,
    Those that were have all but vanished.
  ²⁻⁴ As a result, folk fake flattery face to face,
    Two-faced gossip's the unspoken rule.
  They say "I'll say what I want,"
    "I'm my own person," and
      "Who else do we answer to anyway?"
  ⁷⁻⁸ Because LOVE-less society can really hurt,
    Their messages such a painful reality,
  Infuse our beings, LOVE, with an assurance of utter safety,
    Forever safe from worries about such things.
  LOVE, I'd have you put a permanent stop to it all,
    All this fake flattery and exaggeration—
  Enough is *enough*,
    It's repulsive.

LOVE to me:

⁵ OK, I can see that the poor are being exploited,
    Are crying out for relief.
  Enough *is* enough—I will intervene,
    I want their lives to have the safety they need.

To Diary:

⁶ Gosh, like a fiancée's diamond ring polished a hundred times,
    Like an Olympian's gold-winning performance,
      LOVE's words are so perfect, so flawless.

Psalm 13. Discovering Love in the mirror.

Dear Love, how long will this disconnect last?
    When will I next see you shine that smile back at me?
² How long must I wrestle with my thoughts,
    Feel stressed out and depressed?
There's my true enemy right there,
    But how long will they have the upper hand?

³ Look back at me, my Love, my higher power,
    Put that fire back in my eyes or they'll stick in this lifeless gaze,
⁴ My depression and stress thriving,
    Delighted to crush yet another victim.

⁵ But Love I trust in the fact you never die,
    I feel so excited and alive as you rescue me.
⁶ I'll compose a whole new genre of Love songs
    Because Love has been so, so good to me.

Psalm 14. Party invitation for the exploited.

Idiots mutter to themselves, "Love is fake,
    Moral goodness, just a human construct."
    But look at their lives, full of compromise, morally broken,
        There's such a void of real goodness these days.

² Love peers through the windows of darkened human hearts
    To see if any understand or are genuinely seeking Love.
    ³ But no, it would seem not:
        All darkened hearts seem corrupted,
Each and every one,
    Morally bankrupt, the lot.

⁴ Will the orchestrators of human harm not learn?
    They guzzle the lifeblood out of the lives of Love's people.
Their brains are in their bellies,
    Forgetting the most important thing of all—Love.
    ⁵⁻⁶ And one day they will sit there,
        Starting to sweat, beginning to realize:

        → Decent exploited people
            Have a real sense of Love's presence and power about them,
        → They may be marginalized
            But aren't easily undermined,
        → They're relaxing now,
            Secure in the Love safe house.

⁷ Man! That Love's people would experience that rescue
    Rising up from their sacred space within.
When that happens and their lives are set free,
    Let the parties and celebrations begin!

Psalm 15. The guest list.

Dear Love, who is invited to sit with you?
      Who can live with that sacred presence breathing within them?
² *Anyone* who lives life according to what is right,
    Good, healthy, authentic humans,
        Speaking truth straight from the heart.
³ In other words, it's folk not in the habit of:

    → bad-mouthing others,
    → damaging reputations,
    → generally hurting people.

⁴ Your guests are appalled by moral compromise
    But deeply respectful of followers of Love's daunting path.
You invite people who keep their word—
    Even when it hurts.
⁵ These good people share their resources generously,
    Certainly not profiting from a sense of superiority!
They don't corruptly abuse their influence,
    Extracting some kind of personal gain.

Guests behaving like this are well-grounded indeed.

Psalm 16. Journeying with Love along the path.

Dear Love, you are my higher power,
    I trust you.
² Deep down I whisper:
    "You are completely in charge.
I want to be a good person
    But without you I can forget it."
³ As for the social habits everyone else seems to embrace,
    I have to say my piece:*
⁴ Making shopping, social media, holidays,
    Mortgages, politics, even religion our deeper purpose,
Treating them like *gods*,
    Voilà a recipe for our unhappiness.
That's sure not how I'm going to spend my precious time,
    You won't hear me obsessing about such things.

⁵ Love, you have shown me what is mine to inherit,
    My far safer nourishment, my true me-space.
⁶ I am so lucky to have received this legacy,
    It's so beautiful, so lovely, so *good*.
⁷ Love is amazing (I'll keep on saying it),
    Helping me with my decisions.
At night I feel my Love-filled heart
    Being trained in life's lessons.
⁸ I keep Love clearly in focus
    Because when in that space
        I am not easily fazed.

⁹ Now I am so, so grateful, I feel my core gushing joy,
    My whole body relaxes knowing there is hope.
¹⁰ You won't allow my soul to just rot away,
    For your faithful friend to fall apart.

¹¹ The path ahead is being shown to me—
    Life! Joy!
Love is filling me, such a rush,
    So great to be gathered in this place with you
        For the rest of my days.

  * Or *There are some amazing people in this country, but I would say this:*

Psalm 17. LOVE, saving the real me.

Dear LOVE, hear me out, what I am asking,
    Begging.
  Examine what I am saying, it is legit,
    Completely genuine.
  [2] My integrity holding true,
    May your presence vindicate me.

[3] You don't grant my authenticity easily—
    Especially at night, I've felt you auditing me.
  Result: I haven't intended anyone harm,
    And the things I've said are OK.
  [4] Thanks to what you clarified,
    I have not gone along with exploitative dehumanizing behavior.
  [5] I haven't slipped—
    I've been sticking to LOVE's Way.

[6] So, I am calling in to you, my higher power,
    We must connect—I'm not talking to a wall here!
  [7-9] Wow, I'm still the apple of your eye,
    You still hide us, surround us.
  Amaze me again with your loving nature,
    By how powerfully you shelter me
      From the deadly oppression on all sides.

[10] For there's this LOVE-lessness, burned out compassion,
    Words and tones of voice paying tribute to arrogance,
  [11] That's what's now on my case:
  Watching
  My every move
  From every angle
  Primed to pounce at my slightest mistake and take me down.
  [12] It's like a young stealthy lion,
    Waiting
    Fierce
    Famished
    Poised.

¹³ Love you must rise up here within me,
      As we face them together,
  Bring them down with your clarity,
      Power me out of this danger zone.
¹⁴ Love, reach in and release me
      From the power Love-less people have over me,
  Their goals are short-term,
      Never transcending the day-to-day.
  So, let them have it, let them be "satisfied,"
      On their junk-food, candy-filled life.
  Not just them, but their children,
      Their *grand*children even!

¹⁵ As for me,
      I know I am OK.
  My mind will be satisfied in the morning,
      Seeing your light in my own reflection,
          Knowing Love is alive inside of me.

Psalm 18. We got this!

A poem ascribed to a human finally freed from their demons.

Dear LOVE, I love you! LOVE in me is strength in me.

To Diary:

²⁻³ LOVE is my fixed point of reference,
    My den, my Get-Out-Of-Jail-Free card,
  My higher power, my reliable power source,
    My shield,
  My essential power tool,
    The high ground of my confidence,
      And the one I continue to call.
  Gosh, LOVE is so AMAZING,
    Saving me over and over from all my demons!

⁴ I was drowning in a loveless ocean,
    A fear of death restricting my breathing,
  ⁵ In the midst of an anxiety attack I heard:
    "You're about to die."
  ⁶ I issued my last desperate call:
    "LOVE, you're my higher power," I pleaded,
      "Please: HELP!"
  In the deep and sacred place my rough message landed,
    My gasp was heard.

⁷⁻⁸ And LOVE in me let rip:
    An earthquake hit,
  Shaking my world,
    Even the mountains wobbled.
  It was like this crazy LOVE-anger, angry for me,
    Making my face flush,
  Putting a fieriness in my soul,
    In my eyes.

⁹⁻¹⁵ At this point I imagined LOVE as my superpower—
    I could fly, surfing the wind,
  I could command weather systems,

    Scurrying darkness in the middle of the day,
Causing terrible storms,
    Thunder lurking in the grit of Love's voice echoing through me.
I could shoot arrows and bolts of lightning
    Straight from my fingers.
Scattering fear with my Love superpower,
      I could cleanse the oceans of human trash with a wish,
        Reforest the whole Amazon basin with my breath.
A single blast of Love's breath through me
    Could do all of this and more.
Such is the extraordinary sensation of Love's divine response
    In the deep darkness of the sacred place.

This vision permeated my reality,
    For even though I was drowning,
[16] Love dived in and put its arm around me,
    Back up to the surface, I breathed, and I was *away*.
[17] Away from the toxic relationships,
    Away from their massive influence,
Away from that hatred,
    It was much too much for me.
[18] They tried to crack me again, of course,
    The day I collapsed.
But Love was there once more,
    Strong when I needed it most,
[19] Leading me into a spacious place,
    Rescuing me because Love loves me,
      So much.

[20] Since my conscience has been clean,
    My moral track record agrees,
Love has been such a gamechanger,
    Reaping me dividend upon dividends!
[21] So I am learning to hold,
    Really hold to what Love reveals as right and true.
And I will not compromise
    On that authority within me.
[22] All Love's insights are guiding me,
    Love's instincts becoming my own.

[23] With that clean sheet
    I've been kept from hurting people (myself included).
[24] So a clean conscience, through LOVE,
    Really does reap dividends,
My moral track record does agree
    And LOVE in me has seen it all!

[25-26] For LOVE gives back to what it finds in humans:
    "You are loyal? I am loyal*ty*. With you."
    "You are innocent? I am inno*cence*. With you."
    "You are pure? I am pur*ity*. With you."
But also on the flipside:
    "You are manipulative? I surpass all thought, good luck!"
[27] LOVE's rescue package saves humble people in need of help,
    But also brings proud attitudes crashing to the ground.

To LOVE:

[28] LOVE, for me, you keep me going,
    Brightening even my most dreary or scary day.
    [29] With you on my side I can power through any challenge!
        With you in charge . . . See that vertical wall? WE GOT THIS!

To Diary:

[30] All us humans placing our trust in LOVE
    Are kitted out with LOVE protective clothing,
So yielding to LOVE's way is perfect for us,
    LOVE's words have always proven their worth.
[31] For who or what could we call "God" or our "higher power"
    Except LOVE itself?
Could we ground our lives in anything else
    Even half as solid?
[32] Under LOVE,
    Energy flows through me,
        The way forward is made perfect.
[33] There is such a feeling of lightness and confidence,
    I could literally climb a mountain in five minutes barefoot!
        Up there I'm in my element.

[34] Love awakens my body to face my challenges,
 I'm equipped and ready.
[35-36] Love gives me my smiling shield,
 Signaling liberation.
Love is keeping me going
 With understated authority,
Reinstating my reputation,
 Smoothing my path—
  No more ankle sprain pain games again for me!

[37-38] I'm like a Love cop in the driving seat,
 I chase down the bad guys,
I do not let up
 Until they're all under my arrest.
I take them down and cuff them,
 They can't escape my grip.
[39] Equipped with energy and drive for these challenges,
 Bad vibes cave in to my dynamic authority.
[40] Although they still try to flee the scene,
 I get to neutralize the danger.
[41] They yelp for help but no-one hears them,
 Even Love's keeping quiet.
[42] They get mashed to a pulp,
 Like shredded paper I toss them to the wind.

[43] No longer a hapless victim exposed to attack,
 I am now entrusted with such a senior rank
Even folk I have never met
 Recognize my authority.
[44] There is something about my name
 Now inspiring respect.
So regardless of who I'm facing,
 Even total strangers quickly comply
[45] (The wind taken out from their own sails,
 They are keen to come out of hiding themselves).

⁴⁶ Long live LOVE!
> LOVE rocks!
My safety is restored,
> Hurray for my higher power!
⁴⁷ Its great authority in me compensates for this world's evils,
> Gives me respect from within my circles.
⁴⁸ This is such a win over my rising brokenness,
> This is an airlift rescue
>> From all sudden harm against me.

To LOVE:

⁴⁹ And so LOVE please know, wherever I go,
> Whoever I am with,
I'll never keep quiet about you,
> I am literally singing your praises as I write!
⁵⁰ You are giving extraordinary breakthroughs
> To us your empowered people—
And we get to experience this LOVE,
> Even pass it on to our families,
>> For all generations to come!

Psalm 19. LOVE's loveliness infiltrating me.

Day and night the sky sings of the universe's great beauty,
> The vista proclaims the extraordinariness of creation.
> ^{2} Day after day the view inspires us,
> > Night after night it gives us more perspective.

^{3} Nowhere on the face of the Earth
> Is too remote to tune in to this extraordinary show.
> $^{4-6}$ Nature's great song is reverberating throughout the world,
> > Over continents, oceans, and icecaps.
> In the day the sun takes up its residence,
> > Stepping fourth to welcome its bride the Earth.
> It runs its glorious course from one horizon to the other,
> > Benefitting everything with its warmth.

^{7} LOVE's Way is like it,
> Reviving the soul after a long cold night.
> LOVE's instincts in us can be trusted,
> > Making even uneducated people seem like wise old owls.
> ^{8} LOVE's paths are bang on,
> > Leading to real joy.
> LOVE's words are pure,
> > Putting the fire back in our eyes.
> $^{9-11}$ LOVE's insights are solid,
> > Consistently right.
> Every time LOVE is expressed in us, it is more precious than a home,
> > A beautiful and well-loved home,
> It is scrummier than honey,
> > Than drizzled golden syrup.

Living this way, with these instincts, learning these lessons,
> Following these paths, gaining these insights,
> > We are rewarded brilliantly when we embrace them
> > > And warned of where not to go.

We may also feel daunted—LOVE's total involvement can be daunting!
> This is also normal, healthy.

To Love:

¹² Who is mindful of all their mistakes?
> Some of mine will be hidden from me—purge me!
>> ¹³ Also, Love in me, keep me from intentional harm,
>> May that urge never take root in me.
> Protected from mistakes and intentional harm,
>> I can get that hallowed clean slate,
>>> That precious innocence of any serious wrongdoing.

¹⁴ Love, my inner strength, my saving grace,
> May what I say and the musings of my heart be Love ly.

Psalm 20. May things go well for us.

To Love's people:

When you hit tough times,
    May Love be your answer,
  May that name of our higher power
    Be your defense.
[2] May Love assist you from your sacred safe space,
    Giving you the inner strength you need.
[3] Feel how Love in you is connected
    To all the sacrifices you've made.

Pause

[4] May you see your dreams come true,
    May you find and live out your vocation.
  [5] We will be so happy when we hear of your breakthroughs,
    Proudly flying Love's flag for the occasion.
  May our higher power accompany you,
    Giving you all you know you need.

[6] Now I am certain that Love saves Love's people,
    Answering us powerfully in its expansiveness, its sacredness.
  [7-8] Some people trust in material things,
    Cars, houses, jobs, even weapons—
These folks will be dragged down,
    Down to their knees.
But our confidence is in the name of Love,
    Our higher power.
We will stand back up,
    Reveling in the secure firmness of our footing.

To Love:

[9] Love, help us, may it go well for us,
    Be available when we call for you.

Psalm 21. Smiling champions.

Dear Love, all your champions can't but smile as they draw on you for strength,
> Just so joyful to experience all these breakthroughs!

² You gave them the very thing they are most passionate about,
> Partnering with them 100% to achieve their goals.

Pause

³ You showed up, met them, gave them this golden aura of authority.
> They got to feel seriously "blessed." So good.

⁴ They asked you for help with life right now.
> You've given them not only that,
>> But long and fulfilled lives as well.

⁵ Guided through to awesome solutions by you,
> They attract matching respect and admiration.

⁶ Without a doubt
> They thrive on you permanently,

So unbelievably grateful
> To have you so tangibly present.

⁷ Naturally, they trust in undying Love,
> That gentle but supreme power ruling in them.
>> They're unshakable.

To Love's champions:

⁸ You will decisively overcome all your opposing dark forces,
> You may sense hatred but you are in control.

⁹ So when you feel that darkness,
> That gunk rising up,

The force of Love's passion burning in you
> Will melt your strife;
>> Love eats strife for breakfast!

¹⁰ Evil cannot survive here on Earth,
> Over time and through you,
>> Love will steadily purge it from humanity.

¹¹ Although dark forces were set to break you,
>> They can't follow through.
> ¹² You will make them do a 180 when you aim at them,
>> Aiming Love's laser right in their faces.

To Love:

¹³ Love, it is time you were recognized
> As humanity's greatest strength.
> We will celebrate and party with everything we've got
>> Because of your power pulsating through us.

Psalm 22. Public humiliation and the draft public announcement.

Dear Love, if you really were my higher power,
    Then why do I feel so incredibly alone?!
Why am I still in such dire need of a divine breakthrough?
    Why this cruel indifference to my desperate words?
² You've been my higher power,
    But as I cry out desperately throughout the day
And late on into the night,
    I am faced with nothing but deafening *nothingness*.

³ Yet there you are, unshiftable in your quiet sacred authority,
    The one we promote unreservedly.
⁴ You've always been the one my family has trusted,
    Even my great-great-grandparents relied on you to see them through.
⁵ First, like me, they cried out,
    They trusted;
Yet *they* were saved by you,
    They were not left to feel ashamed.

⁶ The difference is I don't count,
    Folk can't stand me, find me repulsive,
I bug them,
    I am a bug.
⁷ People have spotted me, they are mouthing off at me,
    Shaking their heads condescendingly as if to say:
⁸ "He trusted in 'Love,'
    So ridiculous!
Let 'Love' save Mr. Lovey-Dovey
    If he really is that special!"

⁹⁻¹⁰ Yet ever since the womb
    You've been my higher power!
You were with me at birth
    When I squeezed out through the birth canal.
I was trusting in Love even at my Mama's breast,
    So right from the start this little human counted on you.

¹¹ Be *close* to me, trouble is just too near!
    There is no-one else who can help me.
  ¹² Now I am thrown into a bull pit,
    1-tonne snorting bulls surrounding me.
  ¹³ Their mouths hanging open,
    They gape at me.
There are lions too, roaring, drooling lions,
    Their mouths lined with four-inch fangs.
  ¹⁴ My body is in a strange liquid state of collapse,
    I feel like rubber, a weird stretchy sack of dislocated bones.
My waxy heart is overheating,
    Melting away.
  ¹⁵ With my strength drained, my mouth drier than a desert,
    My tongue sticks to the roof of my mouth.
So is this how it all ends?
    Love laying me down to rest,
        Ashes to ashes, dust to dust?

¹⁶ The show goes on, with the bulls, lions, and now dogs circling me.
    My God, there are people crucifying me!
They are literally piercing me,
    Spiking my hands, my feet!
  ¹⁷ You can see my bones now,
    People are watching transfixed by the unfolding horrors.
  ¹⁸ Since I have been relieved of my clothes,
    People have their eyes on my gear.
Yes I can see them,
    Paper-scissors-stoning for my leather jacket.

¹⁹ Love even now, be close, you are where I draw my strength,
    Quickly come and help me out now!
²⁰⁻²¹ Take me away from this execution scene,
    Empower me to save my precious life from certain fate,
From those snarling dogs,
    From those drooling lions,
        From those wild-eyed bulls with their impaling horns.

²² Then I can speak out again about you
>   To all my friends and circles,
> When we meet and greet,
>   I'll be giving you full credit!

²³ I'll get to say my planned public announcement:

> *"You who feel daunted by Love,*
>   *Sing its praises anyway!*
> *All you folk who have been raised to value Love,*
>   *Grant it special status again!*
> *Give it respect,*
>   *All of you.*
> ²⁴ *Because Love was not disgusted by my turmoil,*
>   *Revolted by the broken human I once was,*
> *You could still see Love shining through my face,*
>   *That I was not abandoned when I begged for help.*

²⁵ These praises are loud and clear,
>   And so it is in your presence,
> Good people, you who still respect Love,
>   That I will keep my promises and join the movement's great work.
> ²⁶ Those under the poverty line will have enough to eat—
>   Nutritious, satisfying food.
> Those who are searching for true Love,
>   Will be free to sing its praises.
> And may life constantly fill you,
>   Your heart of hearts brimming with life forever.

²⁷ *Transcending culture, class, and time, right across the planet,*
>   *Humans will remember and return to Love,*
> *Families everywhere,*
>   *Fully embracing the program.*
> ²⁸⁻²⁹ *For true authority derives from Love,*
>   *Taking over everywhere,*
> *Regardless of socioeconomic contexts.*
>   *It's transcending class:*
> *From the high earners eating and celebrating in Love's honor,*
>   *To the poor at death's door, kneeling to Love.*

⁣³⁰ It transcends time:
   Future generations will still be taught LOVE, *will embrace* LOVE,
³¹ Will declare how LOVE *is just the right way to go,*
   So even those not yet born will learn—

LOVE . . . WORKS!"

Psalm 23. LOVE, my guide, my host.

LOVE is my mountain guide,
    Everything is taken care of.
  ² LOVE takes me alongside quiet lakes,
    And has me stop, rest, and enjoy nature's verdant views.
  ³ My soul drinks it all in,
    Is refreshed.

We move along on exactly the right paths,
    Which is entirely to my guide's credit.
  ⁴ So even when I am led down a dangerous precipice
    In low visibility conditions,
  I will not catastrophize
    Because LOVE is with me.

To LOVE:

Dear LOVE, you know that clickity-click of your walking stick?
    I find its rhythmic pattern deeply reassuring.

⁵ After the long hike ahead you've had prepared
    A handsome hiker's dinner.
  Even though my struggles back home are still present in my mind,
    Your red-carpet hospitality blows my brain.
  You just will not stop topping me up,
    My plate is full,
        My wineglass literally overflowing!

⁶ Wow—Goodness, unshakable LOVE,
    Forever tracking me, my entire life!
  So I'll daily take time just to be
    Present in my sacred LOVE-space
        For the rest of my life.

Psalm 24. Letting go.

Love's jurisdiction is worldwide,
>   Covering the entire planet and everything living here.
>   [2] Love's Land emerged out of a water-filled Earth,
>   Terra Firma out of Water World.

[3] Who can climb into Love's sacred space,
>   Who can go in there confidently standing their ground?
>   [4] Anyone and everyone whose hands are clean,
>   Whose heart is honest.
> Those who do not obsess
>   On society's fake ideals,
> Those who actually do
>   What they say they'll do.

[5] Love saves these people and takes over,
>   They will feel "blessed" and justified.
>   [6] I see a whole generation of people like this coming,
>   Love-hungry,
> Letting Love shine through their faces:
>   Love's people, Lovers through and through.

Pause

[7] So let's let go!
>   I'm letting go of my old battered defensive reflexes,
> I'm opening up.
>   I am letting this glorious authority in.

[8] What or who is this "glorious authority"?
>   Love. Super-effective, mega-powerful, in all my battles.

[9] So let's let go!
>   I'm letting go of my old battered defensive reflexes,
> I'm opening up.
>   I am letting this glorious authority in.

[10] What or who is this "glorious authority"?
> Love. Super-effective, mega-powerful, Love.
> That's what. That's who.

Pause

Psalm 25. My Love GPS, navigating me out of trouble.

¹⁻² Dear Love, I trust you,
>   I'm releasing my entire being into your divine care.

Keep me from feeling embarrassed all the time
>   Like a loser.
>   ³ In fact, no-one who hopes in you, Love,
>   >   Will experience shame
>   (Shame should be and will be
>   >   For unpredictable two-faced behavior).

⁴ So show me *your* ways, Love,
>   Teach me your ins and outs.
>   ⁵ Love, lead me and teach me
>   >   About a life that rings true,
>   Because you, my higher power,
>   >   Are the one who sees me through;
>   Because my hope
>   >   Is constantly grounded in you.
>   ⁶ I won't forget how gracious you are when we make a bad turn,
>   >   So unwaveringly Love-ly—that's just how you've always been.
>   ⁷ I will not, however, allow myself to wallow
>   >   In my old mistakes and rebel tendencies.
>   Undying Love,
>   >   Be true to yourself within me,
>   You are good
>   >   By very definition.

To Love's people:

⁸ So Love is good by very definition,
>   True to course.
>   As a result, Love can correct course
>   >   When we wobble off the beaten track.
>   ⁹ Love is like a GPS for those who admit needing help,
>   >   Showing them the right way forward.

¹⁰ For us who stick to the plan,
   Following the turn-by-turn instructions,
With all the routes suggested being so accurate,
   It's such a kindness to even have it.

To Love:

¹¹ For the sake of your reputation, Love,
   Don't hold my terrible navigation against me.

To Love's *people:*

¹² Who, then, will take this Love GPS dead seriously?
      Good call, you will receive divine directions
         Unique to you.
¹³ Journeying like this pays dividends across the generations,
   Yes, our children also reap immeasurable rewards.
¹⁴ Seriously, Love works transparently
   If you take it seriously
(Details of our binding contract with Love
   Are always fully disclosed).
¹⁵ I'm all-in, constantly refocusing on Love's direction,
   It's my only way to get unstuck and moving again!

To Love:

¹⁶ Come close to me, kindly sit with me.
   I feel lonely,
      I don't feel good.
¹⁷ Lift my mind clear of what's troubling it,
   Relieve my brain's limbic system
      Of its rampant anxiety.
¹⁸ Take stock of my troubled mental state,
   Wipe out the guilt I still feel
For hurting people,
   For undermining your cause.

[19] I cannot believe how many have it in for me,
    They hate me so intensely!
[20] Please,
    Keep my mind safe.
As I trust in LOVE in me,
    Don't let embarrassment take over.
[21] As I'm expecting you,
    May integrity—journeying true to course—
        Safeguard my travels.
[22] LOVE, restore all of us—us, the people you guide,
    On the road to recovery after all our dramas!

Psalm 26. Integrity Trail Path.

Dear Love, show them I'm on track!
    My life trek has been along the Integrity Trail Path.
  Trusting firmly in Love,
    I don't slip up.
² Check me out, run your tests,
    Check my thoughts, what I am feeling deep down—
³ Your loving kindness lives now in my gaze,
    I step out, truth in my stride.

⁴ So I don't hang out with liars,
    I don't spend time with hypocrites.
⁵ To be honest, it's mentally unbearable for me to be there,
    Evacuation is my only option.
⁶ I wash my hands of all that business,
    Gravitating instead, Love, to your deep sacred space in me.
⁷ Then I am ready to speak up: singing your praises,
    Telling people of your beautiful achievements.
⁸ Love, I have always loved sharing your safe house,
    Where your light shines so powerfully within me.

⁹ Please, please, you see my life, my heart?
    Don't let them get flushed down the toilet,
        Into a pit of damaging, reckless behavior.
¹⁰ Lost to dark intentions,
    Driven by personal gain? No thanks!
¹¹ Me, I am trekking on the Integrity Trail Path.
    So Love, please kindly keep me on track.

¹² Right now, my feet firmly placed on solid terrain,
    Joining with all Love's people,
        I'm celebrating Love.

Psalm 27. Strong hearts.

Love is my inner light and my lifeline—
>So who should I be afraid of, really?
>Love is the one holding my entire life together—
>So what should scare me, ultimately?

² When the darkness and pain gain ground,
>Seemingly to gobble me up entirely,
>They will trip up,
>>Wipe out.
>³ Even when threats surround me,
>>My heart will not give ground to fear.
>Even during prolonged battles,
>>My self-confidence holds steady and strong.

⁴ One thing I ask Love,
>It's the only thing I'm really looking for:
>That Love and I may live together
>>Every day of my life,
>Gazing on Love's beauty,
>>Seeking it, finding it,
>In the sacred safe space within,
>>Sensing its rhythm.
>⁵⁻⁶ Because when times get tough
>>(And they will),
>First Love keeps me safe,
>>Hidden away in my Love zen zone.
>I'm then positioned firmly standing tall,
>>Broad perspectives over the challenges I'm facing,
>I'm head and shoulders above,
>>Dwarfing my surrounding troubles.
>I then return to Love's sacred space,
>>Paying tribute with smiles and laughter,
>>>Drumming along to the real Love song rhythms.

To Love:

⁷ Dear Love, listen to what I have to say!
>I don't deserve it but please answer me anyway!

⁸ Deep within my heart
    Reverberates the answer,
"Keep looking for me,"
    Keep finding Love looking back in the reflection.
⁹ Please don't pretend you aren't here
    (Did I frustrate you?)
Honest to God,
    I know you've been there for me,
So please don't cut me loose or abandon me, not now,
    As my higher power you're still my insurance policy!
¹⁰ Even when my parents are not there for me,
    Love always is.
¹¹ Teach me your way of Love,
    Help me feel its smoothness and safety,
        Knowing this straight path is safe from attack.
¹² Please do not—God, no—let me slip
    Into the power of my demons,
Vulnerable to fresh lies against me,
    Accusations of things I never did.

¹³ I have *not* lost hope—
    I *will* get to see the goodness of Love in this lifetime.
¹⁴ Love is on the way.
    While we wait, let us find courage deep down,
Our hearts beating stronger now,
    With Love on the way we can wait.

Psalm 28. Energy resource.

Dear Love, my rock, I'm reaching out to you,
> Please don't play hard-to-get.
If we don't connect, I'll be no better
> Than all the others in their downward spirals.
² So do connect with me as I call in,
> As I reach out,
Voice, emotions, body,
> All straining toward you,
To experience you
> In that deep, sacred place.

³ Don't let me be drawn to harming,
> Destructive, unfair behaving,
Seemingly friendly,
> But boy, with ulterior motives!
⁴ That kind of behavior must be dealt with accordingly,
> Justice has to be served.
⁵ These practices can seem blind to Love,
> To its great achievements.
So that ignorance can knock them for six,
> Never to bounce back.

To Diary:

⁶ Let's celebrate Love,
> It's there for me now I need it.
⁷ Love is my energy resource, my smiling shield,
> So trustworthy, so helpful.
I feel pure joy surging,
> I'm singing along loudly to my favorite Love song.
⁸ For all of us assigned this Love vocation,
> Love is our energy resource, our safe haven.

To Love:

[9] So keep rescuing us Lovers,
      Helping us flourish,
   Being our guide,
      Carrying us our entire lives.

Psalm 29. LOVE's voice, volume turned up to 10.

May all you strong LOVE-filled radiant people
        Now give thanks,
    Give credit back where it's due,
        The source of your strength.
[2] Do remember to give this credit back,
        Say just how awesome LOVE is to you,
    Focus your affections on LOVE,
        Enjoy the beauty of a sacred moment together.

[3-9] LOVE's own voice can be heard
        Over and above scenes of crashing water.
    Like a great God thundering from heaven,
        It's majestic.
    Imagine some oak trees, some of the sturdiest trees there are,
        Yet LOVE's boom shakes and twists them,
    Their strong structures contorted unrecognizably,*
        The branches of the entire forest stripped by the blast.
    And it reverberates on in the great crashing and splintering,
        As one huge old tree finally falls to the forest floor.
    Zooming out, imagining a crazier scene
        As the voice rumbles on:
    Massive land areas jumping about like startled pets,
        A nearby snow-capped mountain is somersaulting!
    LOVE's voice strikes the earth like bolts of lightning,
        Lightning and thunder descend.
    The sheer power of this voice
        Pulsates up too from the ground.
    Feel the sand, the dirt, the rocks in a dry desert,
        All shaken up by the power of the tremor.

In response, all LOVE's people
        Cannot help but cry "Wow!"

[10] The indescribable power of LOVE's impact
        Can flood our imagination,
    Imagining LOVE's great rule
        Powerfully deploying in our lives long term.
    [11] So may LOVE give us LOVERS strength,
        A deep sense of peace and balance.

    * Or *Pregnant deer are so startled they go into labor*

Psalm 30. Dawn never fails.

Dear Love, I'll be singing your praises again;
    You lifted my spirits,
  Wiping off my rivals' grin,
    That smirk from their smug faces.
  [2-3] My mind had sunk
    Into this dark, lifeless funk,
  But somehow you kept me alive,
    Kept me out of Doom Dungeon,
  When I called in for help,
    You fixed me up perfectly.
  Love, you are literally like my God,
    My higher power.

[4] And I'm not alone . . .

To Love's people:

Let all us Love fans
    Be singing Love's praises,
        Remembering and thanking that name.
  [5] Neglecting Love is dire for a while,
    But Love's grace, you see, can be enjoyed a lifetime!
  While our tears at night might feel endless,
    Morning never fails, does it?
        Bringing fresh joy with its light, am I right?

To Love:

[6] I remember when I had everything I needed in life,
    Nothing could faze me, I thought.
  [7] Love, I took your strength
    Totally for granted back then,
  So when I stopped sensing you looking back at me,
    An icy fear of isolation gripped my pounding heart.
  [8] "Please, Love, please,"
    I said out loud, real loud,

⁹ "What good am I to the cause if I fall to pieces?
    How will my chaos sing your praises
        Or guarantee your firm reliability?
¹⁰ Hear me, LOVE, please, I know I really don't deserve it,
    But I so need your help this time!"

¹¹ And boy, was I heard.
    You switched my grieving into full on partying.
You cleaned me up,
    I am glowing with gratitude,
¹² Ready to speak up on how glorious my LOVE is,
    Not silently taking you for granted.
LOVE you're my higher power,
    I'm so, so grateful to you:

Today,

                                                Tomorrow,

                F o r e v e r.

Thank you,

                                                Thank you,

                T h a n k y o u.

Psalm 31. Empowerment for the glass hammer.

In the Love safe house
      I feel safe at last.

Please always keep my thoughts
      From spiraling into a shame black hole—
Now that's what I'd call
      A divine rescue plan!
[2] Love within, I need empowerment now,
      Results ASAP.
May you be as solid as rock under my feet,
      A fortress of safety around me.
[3-4] Yes, Love, you are that rock,
      You are that fortress.
Now lead me, please,
      Guiding me from within,
          Oh yes, you are the only safe path.
For the sake of Love's name,
      Extricate me when my feet fall foul
          Of traps I fail to spot.

[5-6] Pointless obsessions infuriate me—
      I place my trust in Love.
I give you back this life-breath,
      It's yours.
As I do so, Love is already restoring me,
      My true higher power.

[7] Your Loving is so kind and I am so grateful,
      Because you have seen the hell I've been through,
          And my deep-seated anxiety.
[8] Instead of leaving me
      At the mercy of my demons,
I can feel you transporting me
      To a truly spacious place.

[9] Ooze kindness within me, Love, please,
      I am in serious trouble here,
And there's this this heavy sadness,

  Weighing my eyes, weighing my mind, weighing my body.
[10] My whole life's spent constantly regretting,
  Year on year still rehashing my mistakes, my failures.
My energy levels are so low
  I'm like the living dead.
[11] It's bad enough my rivals seeing me as a disgrace,
  But now even my neighbors are so freaked
    They scarper at the sight of me!
      Even my friends are avoiding me!
[12] To be honest, I could die right now,
  No-one would blink,
    I'm about as useful as a glass hammer.
[13] I generate gossip as the local useless outcast
  And fear surrounds me.
At times I'm even convinced
  People are actually scheming to kill me.

[14-15] But I still trust in you, LOVE.
  You are my higher power.
There—I've said it.
  My present and my future are in hand,
So empower me to escape
  From persecution snapping at my heels.
[16] Make this undying LOVE
  Shine through my face,
    Saving me as we beam.

[17] LOVE, please don't embarrass me for trusting in you!
  Instead, reserve embarrassment for human harm.
Silence evil,
  Letting human evil rot in the grave.
[18] Those lips that lie at good people's expense
  Must at some point be silenced,
Zero respect, utter arrogance?
  —We're done here.

[19] Wow, for us who've have taken you seriously,
  The rewards will be so good!

> These benefits will be public so people make the connection:
> > Trust in LOVE = later rewards.
> [20] At first, we lucky ones stake out your secret safe house,
> > Secured against incoming harmful words and plans.
> [21-22] Then, of course, in our panic,
> > We might hit a blip.
> Battening the hatches,
> > Entering lockdown with nowhere to go,
> > > We assume you've nothing to do with our crises.
> But no! Celebrating LOVE,
> > We can see how wonderfully unshakable LOVE is,
> How our voice *is* heard
> > From wherever and whenever we call in on you.

[23] Love LOVE good people!
> Love will have your back if you remain true to its cause.
> But if you grow yourself a proud attitude,
> > You'd better watch out for a full payback.
> [24] All of you empowered by LOVE:
> > Be strong, go for it, chin up!

Psalm 32. Fessing up, unlocking responsibility.

We feel so fortunate when we get the clean slate,
  Our bad choices forgotten,
    Our mistakes off the table.
 ² That's how lucky we are when Love within
  Silences our harsh inner critic,
When our minds clear,
  When we lack that hidden agenda.

³ So here is what not to do:
  At first keeping quiet about my mistake,
I felt constantly exhausted,
  Whining all day long.
 ⁴ My dissonant guilt and Love within
  Sapped my energy like the relentless summer heat.

Pause

⁵ I figured out what I had to do:
  I had to take real responsibility for my mistakes,
No longer pretending
  Like nothing happened.
So I said out loud:
  "I confess my bad choices,
I am so sorry.
  Please may I experience forgiveness."
And that was it!
  I even forgave myself.

Pause

⁶ So, while there is still time,
  I hope that all good people
Lovingly learn to take responsibility,
  Avoiding the judgement deluge disaster.
 ⁷ Love is my hideout,
  Where I am protected from trouble.
 ♪ I am carried by joyful Love anthems,
  Surrounded by songs of my transformation ♪.

Pause

⁸ This is where I'm coming from,
    I've had to learn so much,
  So seeing you and feeling for you now,
    Can I offer the following suggestions:

⁹ Whatever we do,
    Let's not behave like clueless donkeys,
  Needing bits, bridles, and harnesses,
    External controls to correct our course.
¹⁰ Remember too that harmful people
    Have lots of personal issues.
  So let's put our trust in undying LOVE
    And allow that to permeate our lives.

¹¹ Let's choose gratitude and LOVE
    Bubbling up in smiles and restored laughter!
  Sing along, good people!
    We're being remade good as new!

Psalm 33. From Love tunes to worldwide advance.

¹⁻³ Let all us good, joy-beaming people
> Sing beautiful new Love songs!
Gorgeous, multi-layered Love melodies,
> Professionally produced,
Making us all want to shout out . . .
> "I just love this!"
⁴ Why? Because what Love has clarified is so right,
> Love's impact is so profound.

⁵ Love adores justice and goodness,
> The world is filling with its unshakable Loveliness.
⁶⁻⁷ It's the same clarity in Love
> That's behind the entire created order.
Love's influence is massive,
> Like the moon on the ocean's tides,
It's as if the stars themselves
> Were breathed out of its mouth.
⁸ So let all Earth's populations, cultures, and belief systems,
> Take Love with the utmost seriousness,
⁹ Because when Love expresses itself,
> The entire world is made firm and clear.

¹⁰ Love has the power to make nations' Love-less plans useless,
> Render their goals impossible.
¹¹ Love's own plans, however,
> Are rock solid,
And its purposes buried in our hearts
> Carry over from one generation to the next.
¹² Our nations are going to flourish
> With Love functioning as our highest authority,
Our Love-founded communities blossoming,
> Such is the destiny of Love-sworn humanity.

¹³ Love reaches out,
> Sensing all humankind.
¹⁴ It is watchful over all of us,
> From that place deep within,

¹⁵ Shaping each of our receptive hearts uniquely,
>> Mindful of how we act.

¹⁶ No politician is secure by their number of supporters,
>> No activist is safe even by their great influence.
¹⁷ Nothing manmade or powered by us
>> Comes close to making humans safe.

¹⁸ But we do see undying LOVE's gaze in humans,
>> Those who've taken LOVE so seriously,
>>> All the while hoping in its grace.
¹⁹ When times are bleak,
>> It is all that is left keeping their spirits alive.

²⁰ We take the time to sit and wait for LOVE,
>> Equipping ourselves for our day,
²¹ We can feel our spirits soar
>> From that place of trusting in LOVE's sacred name.

²² This is our hope: that undying LOVE
>> Will be *our* undying LOVE.

Psalm 34. Serious long-term joint rescuing.

I'll always be celebrating Love,
    You'll hear me repeating that great name constantly.
    ²⁻³ My heart is so proud
        To be hosting Love.
    If it's a difficult time,
        Hearing this can help us all
            Rediscover that deep smile.
    Let's maximize Love's presence within us,
        Let us celebrate that name *together*.

⁴ This is my story:
    I went looking for Love,
    I felt Love in me awaken,
        Flushing fear clear from my brain.
⁵ Folk who integrate Love are radiant,
    Their faces glow,
    On the External and Internal Shame Scale
        They score a net zero.
⁶ This was the transformation awaiting me
        When I called in my needy state.
    Love awakened,
        My troubles melted away.

⁷ If we've taken Love seriously
        We can picture Love like a camper!
    Camping out in our hearts,
        It transforms our lives.

⁸ Another Love metaphor:
        What do you find most delicious? Chocolate?
    See it? Now take it and taste it—yum!
        Love is that chocolate—sooo good!
    Placing our trust in Love's flavors
        We are fortunate indeed.

⁹⁻¹⁰ So since LOVE ensures we lack nothing truly good,
> Let's live respectfully.
We're not weakened starved wild animals,
> Remembering instead, precious people,
>> LOVE-searching humans lack nothing good.

¹¹ Let me speak to you
> As though you were my own kids,
I am going to share
> About this "taking-LOVE-seriously" business.
¹² Do you love life,
> Each new day offering countless opportunities?
¹³ Then keep from sending destructive messages,
> From speaking deceptively!
¹⁴ Quit doing bad, start doing good,
> Hunt for peace, chase it down!

¹⁵ LOVE sees the world through its good people,
> Listening compassionately to human distress.
¹⁶⁻¹⁸ When alarm bells ring,
> LOVE in us listens,
Whatever the crisis,
> We are empowered, solutions are found.
When hearts and hopes are crushed, broken,
> LOVE knows, draws close, is a safe space.
But a glance at our face will swiftly convey,
> LOVE's zero tolerance for all social evils:
Wherever they might lurk,
> They must be wiped out.

¹⁹ It is terrible how much good people suffer,
> Yet LOVE will completely release them from suffering's throttlehold.
²⁰ Despite the intensity of the trauma,
> With LOVE we discover that *no, we can bounce back.*

[21] Broadly, human evil will eventually fail,
  Will blow up in its own face;
 Justice will be served
  To everything undercutting human goodness.
[22] Meanwhile LOVE's restoration happens deep down
  In the recesses of human hearts,
 Freeing us LOVE followers
  From our fears of being judged.

Psalm 35. LOVE's on their case.

Dear LOVE, come represent us,
> All those in the partnership with me,

Please help us all
> As we take on the negativity we face.

² Shield us, armor-plate us,
> Make your stand with us.

³ Aim your arsenal
> At that darkness pursuing us.

Whisper into our soul:
> Our partnership empowers us to get safely through this.

⁴ Shame on those acting to hurt me,
> Zero respect.

Let them be stopped in their tracks,
> Scratching their heads in confusion,

⁵ Scattered like roaches—
> LOVE's on their case.

⁶ Let them know what it's like to suddenly lose grip,
> Floundering in the dark—
>> LOVE's on their case.

⁷ Don't forget I was manipulated and trapped,
> I'd done nothing wrong!

⁸ Let these actions be brought to rapid ruin,
> May negativity undermine itself for a change.

⁹ I am so happy—right to my core—to be in LOVE,
> I am so glad to be rescued again!

¹⁰ My whole being wants to know:
> Can anything compare to you, LOVE?

You are the strong currency
> Of those with few resources.

You're keeping them secure,
> Safe from exploitation,

From a fate of being stripped
> Of the little they still have.

¹¹ I myself have had series of ruthless witnesses ganging up on me,
    Asking me questions I didn't understand,
¹² Where I tried to do good, I suffered for it,
    Deep sadness entering my soul.
¹³ Unbelievably, these were the same folk I helped,
    When several of them fell seriously sick.
I even turned to religion for them,
    In desperate but unanswered prayer,
I didn't care what people thought,
    So I hunger-struck before God too.
¹⁴ I literally thought they might die,
    I was in a state of mourning,
Stooping, the world heavy on my shoulders,
    As if I were losing a close relative.
¹⁵ Hence my shock, when times got hard for me,
    Those same people I cared for so much,
Were so goddarned pleased!
    Not just one oddball but many of them!
Together, they bad-mouthed me behind my back,
    Day in, day out.
¹⁶ Their mocking tones laced with their bitterness toward me:
    Backstabbers the lot of them.

¹⁷ LOVE in me, how long will you lie dormant,
    Stop my precious life bleeding dry over this—
¹⁸ Everyone will hear just how thankful I am to you,
    My LOVE, how I'll salute you!
¹⁹ So when they high five my bad luck,
    When they hate me for no reason,
When they do that weird wink at me,
    Don't let it get to me.
²⁰⁻²¹ Loudly they lit rip,
    "Hehe, we saw you do it, *Mister*!"
Spitting out allegations
    Right into my face.
The words some people speak
    Are designed to create friction.
They dream up false accusations
    Against good people living good quiet lives.

²² Love, you have seen all this,
>   This is not a time for indifference.
> Make yourself feel close to me,
>   Be my authority.
> ²³ You are my higher power,
>   I surrender entirely,
> Stir your stumps,
>   Vindicate me.
> ²⁴⁻²⁵ May I get the rewards reserved for Love's impeccable goodness!
>   Please don't let the delighted smugness win out,
> Don't let those bullies think:
>   "Result! We got exactly what we were after,"
>   Or, "we had his guts for garters."
> ²⁶ Instead let them be ashamed and confused
>   For feeling delighted at my pain,
> Let them be kicked off their high horse,
>   Stripped of their dignity and exposed.
>   Love's on their case.

²⁷ Meanwhile, may people rooting for my cause
>   Be so glad to see me vindicated,
>   Visibly delighted with the Not Guilty verdict.
> May they always affirm that Love loves its ambassadors,
>   That our well-being is of primary concern.
> ²⁸ Me too—I'll keep on speaking out of how perfect you are,
>   Singing your praises all day long.

Psalm 36. Keep shining, keep resisting.

I am carrying a powerful message,
>	It comes straight from the heart:
Some people no longer understand
>	How seriously important Love is,
You can see its absence
>	In their vacant stare.
² In those eyes you detect self-interest, pride,
>	Blinding them from seeing
>		What they are doing is wrong.

³⁻⁴ When these folk talk,
>	All you hear is twisted versions of the facts.
Not only that,

>	→ They've gotten stuck in unhealthy ways of thinking,
>	→ They've no issue with harmful ideas
>		(Under the cover of night, they plan them out),
>	→ They've forgotten what wise choices are,
>		What doing good in this world means.

To Love:

⁵ Dear undying Love, you exceed all expectations,
>	Your reliability stretches up and out beyond the clouds.
>	⁶ Your goodness towers as tall as mountains,
>		Your justice is deep like the oceans.
Your safety shelters the entire ecosystem,
>	From humans to everything else.

⁷ Undying Love, you are so precious,
>	You're our higher power!
All of humanity may find respite
>	In the confidence-boosting warmth of your embrace.

⁸⁻⁹ In Love our souls experience total satisfaction,
>	As we feast and drink from your extraordinary life source.
And in your light,
>	We see light.

¹⁰ So please keep shining your consistent Loving kindness
> From within us humans who know you,
Radiating your goodness
> From within our hearts now aligned.

¹¹ And please don't let Pride be my kick in the gut,
> Or Manipulation's hand push me away—
¹² Later, we'll see Pride and Manipulation's people:

> → Egos strewn across the ground,
> → Forever brought to their knees!

Psalm 37. Good versus evil.

Two feelings to avoid when dealing with troublemakers:
    1. Worry
    2. Envy
[2] Remember these people have a limited shelf life.
    Picture them like grass,
        Wilting in the withering wind,
            Ready for the chop.

[3-5] Trust in LOVE inside of you,
    Doing good within and around you.
Live your life in this landscape,
    Delighting in LOVE,
        Feeding yourselves daily on its consistency.
If we can just do this work
    Of trusting and dedicating our lives to LOVE,
Then LOVE will make our dreams come true,
    It will actually happen.

[6] Another amazing benefit is being seen
    For the good person you really are,
LOVE's goodness in you
    As clear as the midday sun.

[7-8] Let's talk more about the worrying:
    Stop.
    Yes, some people's exploitation
        Might sometimes lead to "success,"
    But be still now.
        Feel LOVE's presence.
    Paradoxically, worrying is your potential Achilles heel
        Linked to your own hot-headed reactions.
    So let the worrying go,
        It will only make things worse.

[9-10] And our patience pays,
    LOVE helps human beings realize
        The extraordinary potential we were given

(Human harm will one day be unfindable,
  Its shutdown, permanent).
[11] It's the human humility that'll win in the end,
  Just delighted by how peaceful our lives have become.

[12-17] Meantime evil rages on in its fight against good,
  Foaming at the mouth,
Readying its weaponry to wreak havoc,
  Aiming at those with little to their names.
At those leading constructive lives,
  The arsenal is primed and ready.
But LOVE in charge within us
  Confidently smiles at the darkness,
Knowing this season
  Will one day soon be over.
These attacks will seriously backfire
  Right back in evil's face,
Its power source is set,
  Set to fail catastrophically.

The conclusion is obvious:
  I'd rather be on the side of the light
    With little to my name
  Than have all the riches in the world
    But lost to darkness.

LOVE sure has the good guys' backs.

[18] LOVE knows a moral life
  From start to finish.
It generates an inheritance
  That stands the test of time.
[19] So when dark times hit,
  Food shortages hitting the shelves,
Good humans don't feel ashamed,
  Are still satisfied.
[20] Meanwhile, evil and its forces undermining LOVE
  Will be extinguished.
They'll simply burn out
  Like a fire with nothing left to combust.

²¹ While Love-deprived folk borrow,
> Their intentions to repay sometimes cinders and ashes,
Whole-hearted humans get to be generous,
> Not even demanding repayment.
²² Love-inheritors are "blessed,"
> Their resources grow;
Sadly Love-refuters are "cursed,"
> Their access, shut down.

²³ Making Love our delight,
> Our baby steps are becoming confident strides.
²⁴ We still stumble from time to time,
> But Love is always there, helping us back to our feet.
²⁵ I was young once (now I am old!),
> But looking back I can't recall
Upstanding families abandoned,
> Left to beg.
²⁶ No, they are generous,
> Their resources always shared,
>> Their children's futures secure.

²⁷ So quit doing bad,
> Do good instead,
>> Live life to the full!
²⁸ Yes, Love in us loves what is right,
> Will never let us Love-followers go,
But all that is wrong and unfair in this world
> Will one day get shut down.
²⁹ Love will still see
> Its good people's rights fulfilled:
Settling long-term,
> Living a life here we call our own.
³⁰ Wisdom infuses all our words,
> What we say adds up.
³¹ As our footsteps follow our Love-honed instincts,
> We don't slip up . . .

³² Thank goodness,
> For although evil is preying on human goodness,

³³ Love is not leaving its people to such a fate,
    And Love has nothing to do with accusations of "slipping up."

³⁴ Let us keep hoping in Love,
    Keep going in that way.
And we will get the recognition,
    The fulfilling life,
        Which are all ours by right
(Unlike the destructive types,
    They've got it coming to them,
        —You'll see).

³⁵ I say that because it can seem
    Like cutting corners is a shortcut to a vibrant happy life.
³⁶ But I'm telling you I've seen them come, I've seen them go,
    That way gets us nowhere.

³⁷ So look out for those doing good,
    Watch how holistic their lives become.
³⁸ But I'll say it again,
    It'll be game over for rule breakers,
The whole lot of them,
    They're done here.

³⁹ The safe route for us good folk is Love.
    When times are tough, this is where and how we draw our strength.
⁴⁰ Final result? Love wins,
    Freeing us from social evils,
Literally saving us,
    All this because we simply trusted in Love.

Psalm 38. Finding harmony in the dissonance.

Dear Love, my world is shaking, feels like a divine anger,
    Please let me off the hook.
  2-3 It's my guilt and Love clashing within me,
    Darts of dissonance are skewering me.
This dissonant anger is crushing me,
    Sending my body's health into a nosedive.
My body knows my failure,
    My mistakes clashing harshly within me.
4 I'm reliving them all,
    Feeling so overwhelmed by how rubbish I am,
        It's too much.

5 Because I've let this go on too long,
    My failings and stupid decisions have festered.
  6-7 I feel so rough,
    My whole body oozing unhealthiness,
I stoop too much,
    My back's on fire.
All day long,
    My morale levels scrape through the dust,
8 And I feel exhausted,
    Everything about me is broken,
I groan horribly,
    My troubled mind spent.

9 You are my authority,
    You have full access to all my desires and troubles!

10 My heart may be pounding but I'm lethargic,
    Even the sparkle in my eyes is long gone.
  11 I've become repulsive, even to my closest friends,
    My neighbors are also keeping their distance.
  12 As for those trying to trap me, hurt me, take me down,
    They go on and on,
Planning and scheming my looming fate
    And how to trick me into it.

¹³⁻¹⁶ But I am blessed with a kind of deafness,
> I can't hear a thing.
With a kind of muteness
> I'll keep schtum.
In case they smirk at my next crisis,
> These ears, this mouth:
>> Out-of-Order.

To *you*, Love,
> I speak up,
I am waiting, hoping for you,
> You hear, you listen,
You're in charge here,
> You're my higher power.

¹⁷ My next crisis is lurking
> Just around the corner,
My pain,
> Simmering away.
¹⁸ This time it's linked to wrong things *I* have done
> And I'll state them publicly.
I am distraught by them,
> The harm *I* have caused.
¹⁹ Meantime, my enemies have multiplied,
> Ruthlessly blowing everything out of proportion,
They hate me—
> My bad choices don't make me a bad *person*.
²⁰ They're after me because I'm still about the good cause
> And they're all about making the good guys pay.

²¹⁻²² So please don't let me down, Love,
> You're my higher power!
Stay close. Come quick. Help. You're in charge here.
> You're the one who helps me through these crises!

Psalm 39. Vanishing vapor.

To Diary:

I kept thinking, "I need to watch my steps and my mouth,
    Any damage is on me.
    So when those up-to-no-good-guys are around,
        I must especially watch what I say."
   2-3 I became so fixated on this,
    I said nothing at all, good or bad.
I felt terrible,
    My heart pounding,
Even when meditating,
    I was as calm as a raging fire.

So I broke my silence . . .

To LOVE:

⁴ Dear LOVE, I need to know how my life ends up,
    What this small life will be worth,
        To understand my own fragility!
⁵ My time here next to your permanence
    Amounts to nothing.
Even at our most promising moments
    We humans are but vanishing vapor trails.

Pause

⁶ Surely we all go about our business like unthinking robots,
    Pointlessly, we stuff our lives full,
Full of fleeting activities and stuff,
    Hoarding what we can't even take with us.

⁷ LOVE, you're in charge,
    So what am I waiting for?
It's time to place my hopes
    Under your jurisdiction.
⁸ Save me from my mistakes,
    Please don't let me look ridiculous,
        Silly to those who don't understand.

⁹ So again, I'm not making a sound, keeping my mouth shut,
    I'm letting you do all the talking . . .

¹⁰ . . . And the stopping!
    Please stop these catastrophes you've let reach me!
I am crumbling,
    Knocked for six by this blasting power.
¹¹ And when we don't live right,
    We pay the price, you correct,
You reveal how everything once so precious to us
    Is actually worthless,
How we humans
    Are but vanishing vapor trails.

Pause

¹² So hear my deepest heart wish, Love,
    I'm checking in with you in desperation,
        I need to feel you with me in my tears—
I sometimes feel like a stranger,
    Like all those who've gone before me
        The earliest pioneers into Love's Land.
¹³ And can you please give my mind a break
    From the intensity of your gaze?!
So I can gently start rebuilding this short life,
    Before I go and kick the bucket?!

Psalm 40. LOVE's rescue made available in its own time.*

A while back, I was desperate for immediate results:

¹¹⁻¹² Dear LOVE, don't hold back on gentle kindness to me,
    Your constant LOVING action, your truth—
They protect me from surrounding, overwhelming trouble.
    My heart misses a beat,
My eyes open at last,
    I can't believe all the damage I've caused.
¹³ Please, my LOVE, rescue me,
    Come *quickly* and help me just in time!

¹⁴ Make it happen so everything aimed at breaking me,
    Will be sunk in shame and confusion,
All darkness sent my way,
    Driven back, exposed.
¹⁵ Let any sniggering at my expense
    Be ashamed by the sheer ridiculousness of sniggering.
¹⁶ At the same time,
    All us folk with hearts set on LOVE
Should be beaming with joy and thanks,
    Loving being made to feel safe
And singing as one:
    ♪ 'LOVE So Amazing!' ♪

¹⁷ Seeing all that,
    Seeing my beggar status,
My awareness of you my help,
    My divine rescuer:
Be present!
    Right now!

. . .

---

* Chronological ordering. Cowritten with Kirk Woodyard.

Today:

¹ In the end, I've learned I must wait on Love *patiently*.
    Eventually it arose within me in response to my cries.
  ² As it arose, so did I, breaking through,
    Free from my slimy pit of horridness,
Placing my feet on far firmer ground,
    Walking now with self-assured strides.
³ Whistling and singing along to a new tune,
    I'm so grateful the wait was worth it,
        The holding-on for Love's divine breakthrough.
Many hearing of these kinds of transformation
    Grasp the utter respect and reassurance
        Trusting in Love gives:
⁴ Trusting in Love
    + Avoiding pride
    + Indifferent to society's lies
    = Flourishing humans.

⁵ Love, you are my higher power!
    The change you bring is huge, amazing,
        Your focus on people absolute.
I literally cannot summarize everything you have changed,
    Nothing compares.
⁶ So although deaf to it before,
    I've got it at last:
You just keep on steadily giving,
    No payment needed!

⁷⁻⁸ This time I simply said, "OK, here I am."
    And my biography was written for me and in me,
Emblazoned across my heart:

        "Love's Way:
  Acting with Love as My Higher Power Brings Me Pure Joy."

⁹ Now in my most important meetings
    I speak up about this great news,
        This restored pure life.

You know me, Love,
>   I can't shut up about you!
¹⁰ I'm not being vague about your goodness—
>   It's so dependable, it's our path to safety,
>> I have to go on the record about this!
You, your Loving action, your reality,
>   It's all on full display here
>> And to everyone listening in.

Psalm 41. When body, mind, and reputation are under attack.

To Love's people:

Taking care of the underprivileged through hard times—
    Such a good investment.
  When hardships come knocking on our own door,
    Love sees us through too.
²⁻³ Not only will Love keep our head above water,
    Or protect us from intentional harm,
        Or even restore and re-energize us when we're sick,
    But we'll actually flourish in the place we settle.

⁴ I said to Love, "Please let me off the hook,
    Make me whole again even though I've failed you."

⁵ I know some have it in for me:
    When will I just disappear for good?
  When will my name be forgotten?
    They want to know!
⁶ If they come to visit,
    I'll get the usual social niceties,
Although what they're really after is fodder,
    Fodder for their immediate gossip campaign.
⁷ And so it will go, the hateful whispers,
    How best to hurt me?
⁸ "He has an infection, he'll never recover," they'll say,
    "He'll never be getting up again," they'll mutter.

⁹ Even my very closest friend—we did life together!—,
    Became a Judas to me.

To Love:

¹⁰⁻¹¹ But, Love, please forgive me my mistakes,
    Pick me up, let's show them:

    1. Love's great pleasure so strong within me
    2. Targeting the weak has failed!

¹² You're sustaining me now in a place of integrity,
    That presence and smile of Love is within me forever.

¹³ I celebrate you, Love,
    Higher power for all your people!
  Always have been, always will be!
    Yes, yes, and yes!

Appendix: "Accurate" Bible Translations

WHEN WE THINK ABOUT the vocabulary to use in rendering ancient poetic texts like the Psalms, there is usually a wider conversation to be held about "accuracy," which is sometimes described as "getting as close to the original text as possible" (NIV).

However, what is not often sufficiently grasped is that for a generation spiritually curious yet allergic to religious vocabulary, translators sticking to their guns on words like "merciful," "rebuke," and "Lord" can distance the texts further and further from that place of resonating discovery many people long for, both outside and inside the church.

One reason suggested for the confusion around accuracy is to understand the contribution of translated religious texts to the task of preserving that which is sacred.[1] *Love Letters* should therefore not be perceived as an attempt to play fast and loose with God's holy message, but rather to develop Saint Paul's idea that the ancient insights really are for the benefit of everyone. Of course, if those words and sentences were originally written in a deliberately religious and historical style, then maybe "accuracy" would mean attempting some kind of trade-off between old religious English equivalent terms and natural English expression. But what if the words at the time were not alien to mainstream linguistic usage? What if the wording was contemporary and made a real impact? Would translating the texts now in a patently religious and archaic style perhaps even be guilty of introducing a measure of distortion and distance to many of today's readers? Is the context as sacred as the text?

For decades, bible translation has begun understanding the nature of its work as an intricate balancing act with admittedly no perfect solution.

---

1. Bainbridge, John T. "Translating Κύριος after 600 Years of 'the Lord's' Faithful Service," *The Bible Translator* 71.3 (2020) 337–339.

Appendix: "Accurate" Bible Translations

But until now, and as dramatic and profound as they must have seemed, the discussions and choices have largely been around quite specific issues, such as gender neutrality ("dear brothers *and sisters*").

However, dependent on the purpose of the translation, some of the central English vocabulary for many readers may urgently need to evolve too if the translations are to remain "accurate" for them.[2] It is argued here that—perhaps more than in any other biblical book—the Psalms offer us a sincere invitation for more contextualized renderings because they were so deeply contextualized at the time and were so rich in relevant metaphor, at least on one level. Surprisingly, buried not too deeply, right here in the Psalms are clear pointers to core ideas that people today—biologically identical of course to our ancestors 3000 years ago—know only too well, such as responsibility, empowerment, partnership, success, failure, authenticity, ecology, reality, manipulation, brokenness, confusion, and much more. So, the great continuity between that ancient Hebrew culture and our own lies in the Psalms' presentation of the rugged spirituality of the human condition. This too must be communicated carefully between these two very alien cultures.

To develop a more thorough understanding of accuracy, the notion of equivalence cannot be long avoided. Translation theorist and pioneer Eugine Nida states that equivalence rests on "the relationship between receptor and message [being] substantially the same as that which existed between the original receptors and the message."[3] Equivalence, then, is about exploring how to reflect that relationship as accurately as possible in the target culture.

The modern non-religious reader is indeed a culture unto itself. It does not speak Bible-speak, it does not believe in a monotheistic supreme creator called "the Lord,"[4] and frankly it probably never will. What we hope here is simply to have restored a little of the resonance, connection, and transformation that must have initially sent the Psalms on their timeless voyage through history, across the entire planet, to a readership now including the religiously indifferent or skeptical.

---

2. This could also be said for other languages with long histories of Bible translation.

3. Nida, Eugene A. *Towards a Science of Translating: With Special Reference to Principles and Procedures Involved in Bible Translating* (Leiden: Brill, 1964), 159.

4. It should be remembered of course that the notion (and motion) of letting go to Love's higher authority is consistently represented throughout.

Printed in Great Britain
by Amazon